Little People, BIG DREAMS™
ANNA PAVLOVA

Written by
Maria Isabel Sánchez Vegara

Illustrated by
Sue Downing

Frances Lincoln
Children's Books

One frosty morning, in Saint Petersburg, Russia, a little girl called Anna was born. She arrived two months early and was such a tiny baby that doctors feared for her life. But despite her delicate health, her spirit was strong.

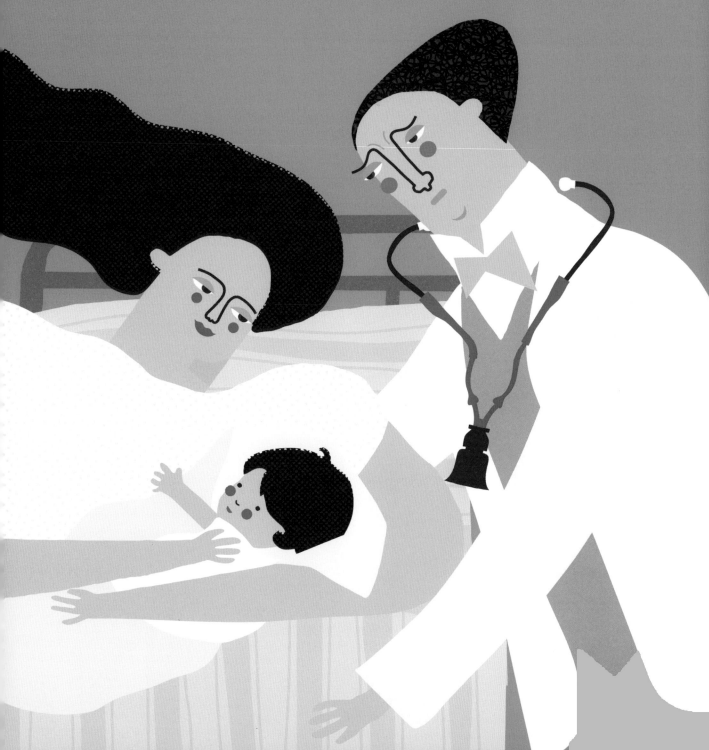

Anna lived in a tiny house on the outskirts of the city. Her father died while she was still small, and her mother worked from dawn to dusk to bring food to the table— and a present for her daughter every now and then.

One day, her mother announced that they were going to the Mariinsky Theater to watch a ballet called *The Sleeping Beauty*. Gazing at the prima ballerina floating on her tiptoes, Anna knew that dancing was all she wanted to do.

From that moment on, every thought she had was of ballet! She begged her mother to take her to lessons, and two years later, when Anna was ten, she was accepted at the Imperial Ballet School, the best in the world at the time.

Most teachers thought her feet were too bent, her ankles too thin, and her arms too long. Even her fellow students called her "Little Savage!" But Anna kept practicing night and day. She knew that only hard work transforms talent into genius.

Her official debut was at the Mariinsky Theater, the place where she had discovered ballet. She wasn't as strong or athletic as the other dancers, but she moved with such delicacy, lightness, and grace that the audience couldn't take their eyes off her.

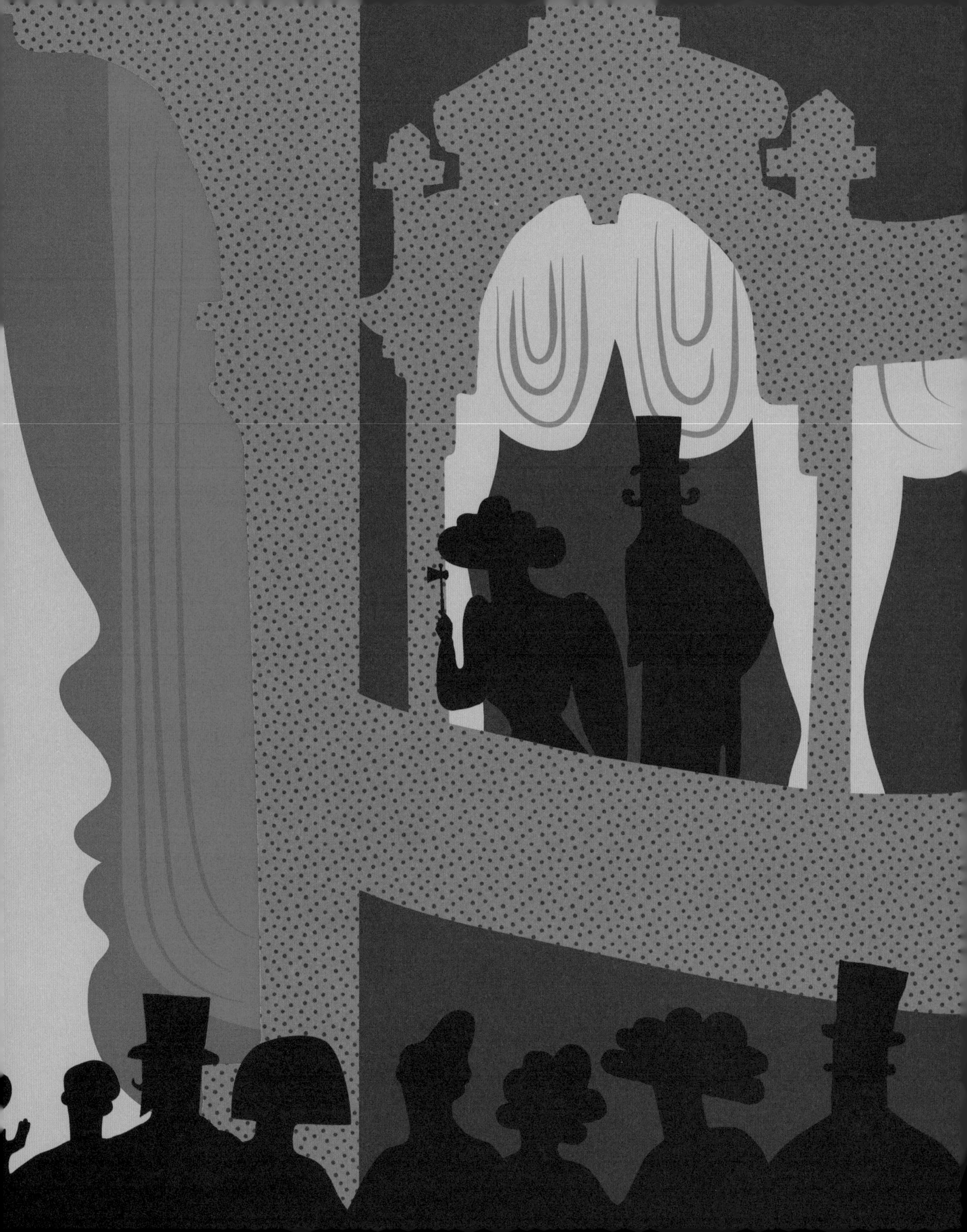

When she danced *The Dying Swan*, it became her most acclaimed performance. The ballet lasted less than four minutes, but Anna danced with such emotion that it was enough time to touch everybody's hearts.

Soon, she was announced as the prima ballerina at the Imperial Ballet, one of Russia's treasures.

PAVLOVA

She became its most precious jewel—a superstar
with legions of fans who called themselves Pavlovatzi.

The following year, she left Russia and toured Europe
for the first time. After her performance in the Swedish
city of Stockholm, crowds gathered at her hotel.
To their delight, Anna threw flowers from her balcony.

Anna joined the prestigious Ballet Russes, which became the greatest sensation in Europe. Yet, after their first season in Paris, she felt it was time to start her own company and bring ballet to places where it had never been seen before.

With the Pavlova Company, Anna became the first ballerina to tour the world. Wherever she performed, from New York to Egypt, people felt moved. And after war broke out in Europe, she helped Russian orphans find new homes.

Back in England, where she lived, Anna mixed ballet with dances she had learned in Japan and India.

She also opened her home studio to a new generation
of dancers eager to learn from one of the greatest.

And living a life devoted to ballet, little Anna—the world's most beloved ballerina—learned something incredible: true success doesn't lie in the applause of others, but in the accomplishment you feel every time you give your best.

ANNA PAVLOVA

(Born 1881 – Died 1931)

1899

c.1920

Anna Matveyevna Pavlovna Pavlova was born in Saint Petersburg, Russia.
When she was eight, her mother took her to see *The Sleeping Beauty* at
the Mariinsky Theater. Anna was captivated and became determined to
learn ballet. Within two years, she was accepted at the Saint Petersburg
Imperial Ballet School. She wasn't a natural dancer and she was called
names by other children, but she practiced hard to improve her technique
and trained under renowned teachers like Christian Johansson, Pavel
Gerdat, and Nikolai Legat. Anna graduated at just 18 years old and went
on to star in the production *La Fille Mal Gardée* at the Mariinksy Theater.
In 1905, Anna performed as the lead solo dancer in *The Dying Swan*.
It became the most iconic performance of her career, and soon after

1925   1929

Anna was named as a "prima ballerina." This meant that she was the primary female dancer in the Russian Imperial Ballet. Accompanied by other dancers, Anna began to tour abroad and gained recognition across the world. In 1911, she created her own ballet company and put her husband, Victor Dandré, in charge of organizing her tours. For the final two decades of her ballet career, she traveled all over the world, inspiring young children and adults to fall in love with ballet. She covered over 350,000 miles on her tour, visiting cities within North America, South America, Asia, Africa, Europe, and more. Anna, the most famous prima ballerina of all time, danced her way into the history books and the hearts of many.

Want to find out more about **Anna Pavlova?**

Have a read of this great book:

Swan: The Life and Dance of Anna Pavlova by Laurel Snyder

Brimming with creative inspiration, how-to projects, and useful information to enrich your everyday life, quarto.com is a favorite destination for those pursuing their interests and passions.

Text © 2022 Maria Isabel Sánchez Vegara. Illustrations © 2022 Sue Downing
Little People Big Dreams and Pequeña&Grande are registered trademarks of Alba Editorial, SLU for books, publications and e-books. Produced under licence from Alba Editorial, SLU.
First Published in the USA in 2022 by Frances Lincoln Children's Books, an imprint of The Quarto Group.
Quarto Boston North Shore, 100 Cummings Center, Suite 265D, Beverly, MA 01915, USA
Tel: +1 978-282-9590, Fax: +1 978-283-2742 www.Quarto.com
All rights reserved.
No part of this publication may be reproduced, stored in a retrieval system, or transmitted, in any form, or by any means, electrical, mechanical, photocopying, recording, or otherwise without the prior written permission of the publisher or a licence permitting restricted copying.

This book is not authorised, licensed, or approved by Anna Pavlova.
Any faults are the publisher's who will be happy to rectify for future printings.
A catalogue record for this book is available from the Library of Congress.
ISBN 978-0-7112-7112-8
Set in Futura BT.

Published by Peter Marley • Designed by Lyli Feng
Edited by Lucy Menzies and Claire Saunders • Production by Nikki Ingram
Editorial Assistance from Rachel Robinson
Manufactured in Guangdong, China CC072022
1 3 5 7 9 8 6 4 2

Photographic acknowledgements (pages 28-29, from left to right): 1. (Eingeschränkte Rechte für bestimmte redaktionelle Kunden in Deutschland. Limited rights for specific editorial clients in Germany.) Anna Pavlova,Anna Pawlowa (*12.02.1881-23.01.1931+) , Ballettänzerin, Tänzerin (Ballett); Russland (UdSSR), - Primaballerina des ehem. Kaiserlichen Hofballetts Petersburg, - o.J. © ullstein bild via Getty Images. 2. Russian ballerina Anna Pavlova with a swan at her home in London, circa 1920. She is most recognised for her role in the Dying Swan, written for her by choreographer Mikhail Fokine, which she performed more than 4000 times © Popperfoto via Getty Images. 3. 11/30/1925-France: Our pictures show the famous dancer Madame Anna Pavlova rehearsing at the theatre Des Champs Elysees where she will give some new interpretation of her famous dances. It is said that the booking for the first three performances has been entirely sold out © Bettmann via Getty Images. 4. Anna Pavlova, prima ballerina of the Imperial Theatre in St Petersburg in London 1929 © Everett Collection Historical via Alamy Images

Collect the Little People, **BIG DREAMS**™ series:

FRIDA KAHLO	**COCO CHANEL** 	**MAYA ANGELOU**	**AMELIA EARHART** 	**AGATHA CHRISTIE** 	**MARIE CURIE**	**ROSA PARKS** 	**AUDREY HEPBURN** 

EMMELINE PANKHURST	**ELLA FITZGERALD**	**ADA LOVELACE** 	**JANE AUSTEN**	**GEORGIA O'KEEFFE**	**HARRIET TUBMAN**	**ANNE FRANK**	**MOTHER TERESA** 

JOSEPHINE BAKER 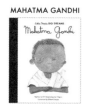	**L. M. MONTGOMERY**	**JANE GOODALL**	**SIMONE DE BEAUVOIR** 	**MUHAMMAD ALI** 	**STEPHEN HAWKING** 	**MARIA MONTESSORI**	**VIVIENNE WESTWOOD**

MAHATMA GANDHI	**DAVID BOWIE**	**WILMA RUDOLPH** 	**DOLLY PARTON**	**BRUCE LEE** 	**RUDOLF NUREYEV** 	**ZAHA HADID** 	**MARY SHELLEY** 

MARTIN LUTHER KING JR.	**DAVID ATTENBOROUGH**	**ASTRID LINDGREN** 	**EVONNE GOOLAGONG** 	**BOB DYLAN**	**ALAN TURING** 	**BILLIE JEAN KING** 	**GRETA THUNBERG** 

JESSE OWENS	**JEAN-MICHEL BASQUIAT**	**ARETHA FRANKLIN**	**CORAZON AQUINO**	**PELÉ**	**ERNEST SHACKLETON**	**STEVE JOBS**	**AYRTON SENNA**

LOUISE BOURGEOIS	**ELTON JOHN**	**JOHN LENNON**	**PRINCE** 	**CHARLES DARWIN**	**CAPTAIN TOM MOORE**	**HANS CHRISTIAN ANDERSEN**	**STEVIE WONDER**

MEGAN RAPINOE

MARY ANNING

MALALA YOUSAFZAI

ANDY WARHOL

RUPAUL

MICHELLE OBAMA

MINDY KALING

IRIS APFEL

ROSALIND FRANKLIN

RUTH BADER GINSBURG

MARILYN MONROE

KAMALA HARRIS

ALBERT EINSTEIN

CHARLES DICKENS

YOKO ONO

MICHAEL JORDAN

NELSON MANDELA

PABLO PICASSO

AMANDA GORMAN

GLORIA STEINEM

FLORENCE NIGHTINGALE

HARRY HOUDINI

J.R.R. TOLKIEN

ELVIS PRESLEY

NEIL ARMSTRONG

ALEXANDER VON HUMBOLDT

NIKOLA TESLA

WILMA MANKILLER

MARCUS RASHFORD

LAVERNE COX

MAE JEMISON

DWAYNE JOHNSON

HELEN KELLER

ANNA PAVLOVA

QUEEN ELIZABETH

ACTIVITY BOOKS

STICKER ACTIVITY BOOK

COLORING BOOK

LITTLE ME, BIG DREAMS JOURNAL

Discover more about the series at www.littlepeoplebigdreams.com